Best Practices in Community Conscious Policing:

A Reflection on Law Enforcement Community Building Workshops

by

Training 4 Transformation, LLC
www.Train4Transformation.com

Author: Brandon Lee, MAT

Edited by: Hun Taing, MA and Theresa Anderson, MA
Date of Publication: August 22, 2016

Community Conscious Policing™

A Culturally Competent, Equitable and Empathetic approach to law enforcement Based on 21st Century Conscious Leadership principles (T4T curriculum)

This report is highly recommended for continuing education in law enforcement, students in criminal or social justice related fields, advocates involved in police accountability and organizations seeking to increase their outreach capacity by collaborating with local law enforcement agencies.

FBI National Academy Associates Annual Spring Training 2015

First published by Dog Ear Publishing
4011 Vincennes Rd
Indianapolis, IN 46268
www.dogearpublishing.net

ISBN: 978-1-4575-4483-5

This book is printed on acid-free paper.

Printed in the United States of America

Thoughts 2 Reality
Book Writing Services

www.thoughts2realitybooks.com

About the Book:

The polarization of law enforcement and community members deepens as our nation continues to erupt into national protests and states of emergency in Ferguson, Baltimore, New York, Cleveland, South Carolina, Florida, Minnesota and Chicago after a flurry of unarmed residents were killed by law enforcement. Trust has been broken, the police are scared, communities are unsafe and protests erupting. We know the problem. The question is, ***"What is the solution?"***

Join Training 4 Transformation, LLC in <u>Best Practices for Community Conscious Policing</u> as we delve beneath the controversy to discover our shared humanity between law enforcement and community.

The goal and purpose of T4T is to "*Humanize our collective experiences and bring others together who may otherwise remain at a perpetual distance.*"

Dedication

"It takes a village to raise a child."

This book is Dedicated to my loving wife, son and twin daughters. Thank you for believing in Papa, my world begins and ends with you!

To my mentors, both professional and personal, your efforts, time, wisdom and invaluable experience are truly appreciated. I am eternally grateful for my extended family in Texas, Delaware, Vermont, Oregon, Mexico, Spain and Cuba to name a few.

Most especially, I would like to honor my family in Oakland, California who thoroughly prepared me for this game called life. My grandmother, our matriarch, is the only person whose opinion truly matters to me. Thank you for your sacrifice, compassion and eternal support. I hope we made you proud.

In loving memory of my father James William Lee and grandfather Jimmy Edwin Rowe who each stood up in the face of adversity so I that could sit down.

It's our turn now...

Dedication

Lt. Jonathan Hall
of the Wilmington Police Department

A percentage of the proceeds from this book will be donated to the Jonathan Hall Fund to support Lt. Jonathan Hall of the Wilmington Police Department in Delaware who is valiantly fighting against Leukemia.

He is married with two loving children, a member of Alpha Phi Alpha Fraternity, Inc. and served as past master of Union Lodge #21 (PHA) in Wilmington, DE. Mr. Hall represents the epitome of community conscious policing and taught me what it truly means to be a peace officer.

He is loved and respected by all, law enforcement and community alike. Thank you for your service and sacrifice, get well soon Noble!

Acknowledgements

Thank you to the Department of Public Safety Standards and Training in Salem, Oregon, FBI National Academy Associates Oregon Chapter, the City of Corvallis Police Department and City of Corvallis Mayor Julie Manning for supporting our Law Enforcement Community Building Workshops centered on Best Practices in Community Conscious Policing.

Most especially, we would like to acknowledge and thank the hundreds of community members and organizations who volunteered their time, traveled and participated. Finally, it would not have been possible without the talented Training 4 Transformation, LLC facilitation team, staff and volunteers who are bilingual, trained in experiential learning, lived or worked internationally all while maintaining local roots in their respective communities.

Below are a few of the law enforcement agencies, community organizations and cities who contributed to an unprecedented statewide event. Your collective efforts are truly appreciated:

Law Enforcement Organizations

1. FBI National Academy Associates, Inc.
2. Corvallis Police Department
3. Portland Police Bureau
4. Woodburn Police Department
5. Federal Bureau of Investigation
6. Salem Police Department
7. Independence Police Department
8. Milton-Freewater Police Department
9. Washington County Sheriffs Office
10. Mount Angel Police Department
11. Marion County Sheriffs Office
12. Keizer Police Department
13. Vancouver Police Department
14. Oregon State Police
15. Tigard Police Department
16. Springfield Police Department
17. Forest Grove Police Department
18. Eugene Police Department
19. Klamath Falls Police Department
20. Beaverton Police Department
21. Benton County Sheriffs Office
22. Lake Oswego Police Department
23. Gladstone Police Department
24. Gresham Police Department
25. Tillamook Police Department
26. Newport Police Department
27. Clackamas County Sheriff
28. Hillsboro Police Department
29. Clatsop County Sheriffs Office
30. North Plains Police Department
31. Lebanon Police Department

Community Organizations

1. National Women's Coalition
2. National Association for the Advancement of Colored People (NAACP)
3. Community Citizen Board
4. Cambodian Association
5. Small Business Owners
6. Latino Police Commission
7. Faith Based Organizations
8. Boystrenth Program
9. Safe Haven
10. Mano a Mano
11. Homefree
12. Visioning and Partnership
13. Homeless Activities
14. Roosevelt High School, Portland
15. Portland Community Police Collaborative
16. Vancouver Police Department Chief's Diversity Advisory Board
17. League of United Latin American Citizens (LULAC)
18. Corvallis Ancient Free and Accepted Masons
19. MW Prince Hall Grand Lodge of Oregon, Idaho and Montana Inc.
20. Center for Intercultural Organizing
21. Woodburn City Council
22. Knight Vision Security

Cities of Community Participants

1. Portland
2. Vancouver, WA
3. Lane County
4. Salem
5. Lake Oswego
6. Eugene
7. Hillsboro
8. Woodburn
9. Corvallis / Albany
10. Beaverton

Table of Contents

SECTION I Data Collection
Context:
- Oregon Demographics of Residents

Problem:
- Biased Policing / Excessive Force / Racial Profiling / Erosion of Communal Trust / Liabilities

Process:
- Listening Sessions Report – A Community and Police Partnership to End Racial Profiling
- Decreasing Crime by Increasing Involvement
  - A Guidebook for Building Relations in Multi-Ethnic Communities
- Key to Successful Community Policing

Next Steps:
- Training 4 Transformation, LLC

SECTION II Who are we?
Introduction
- Community Conscious Policing Workshop
- Workshop Objectives

SECTION III What do we do?
City of Corvallis Police Department Community Building Workshop
Press: *"Crossing the Color Lines: Police & Citizens Talk through Tough Issues"*

Executive Summary

The polarization of law enforcement and community members deepens as our nation continues to erupt into national protests and states of emergency in Ferguson, Baltimore, New York, Cleveland, South Carolina, Florida and Chicago after a flurry of unarmed Black, Latino, Native and mentally challenged people were killed by police officers. These violent episodes are manifestations of our legacy of the suppression of communities of color by state powers. Trust is broken, the police are scared, communities are unsafe and protest erupting. We know the problem. The question is, "What is the solution?"

As a Black man who spent most of my life and energy fighting law enforcement on racial profiling cases, I believe it has become my calling to pave a proactive and preventative path to saving lives, reducing violence and liabilities. Everyone is talking about community policing but not many are doing it and those attempting are not doing it well enough. We wanted to build upon the current state of community policing to something deeper, more comprehensive and authentic. What is missing and needed is transformation, specifically the opportunity to transform community relationships with law enforcement.

Consisting of activists, advocates, educators, conflict transformation specialists, trained facilitators and bridge builders, my wife and I founded Training 4 Transformation, LLC in Portland, Oregon to create opportunities for communities and law enforcement to engage in authentic dialogue. Conflict Transformation Specialists like my wife knows that until we begin to do the work on healing broken or wounded relationships, we will continue to have direct violence. Our agency specializes in equity-focused community building. The foundation of our work is to create opportunities where community members and police officers can authentically listen, share, learn and connect through humanizing our respective experiences, thus transforming the current interpersonal and intercultural relationships.

We started in the beautiful college town of Corvallis, Oregon. Working in partnership with the City of Corvallis Police Department and NAACP Corvallis branch, we delivered an unprecedented Community Building Workshop where the entire Police department had the unique opportunity to engage with local community members confronting issues of profiling, stereotypes and prejudice. The workshop exceeded the police officers and community member's expectations. More importantly, the workshop was transformative. Chief Jon Sassaman replied in our evaluation, *"Your depth of understanding of the contemporary issues and ability to present the subject in such an interesting and profound way produced one of the most memorable training experiences in our department's history."* The training was featured in the Gazette Times, "Crossing the Color Lines: Police, Citizens Talk through Tough Issues (2014)."

For activists and advocates, cultivating relationships with police departments yield many benefits for the community. I had the privilege of being invited by Chief Jon Sassaman and his leadership team to participate in their oral review board evaluations. These interview panels gave me valuable insight to the standards and rigor of their hiring process. Each time I participated, nearly 100% of the candidates we recommended were hired and retained through the police academy. I served as a community member on panels that consisted of university officials, senior officers, business and local community representatives, students and neighbors. Corvallis PD has regularly qualified for the prestigious CALEA accreditation, which is considered to be the gold standard in public safety.

Our success in Corvallis lead to an opportunity to host a second community building workshop; however this time, at the state level. *"At the request of the FBI National Academy Associates, Brandon and Hun Lee implemented their innovative Training for Transformation model to moderate key discussions between law enforcement and community members throughout the day. Attendees discussed a wide range of issues and concerns, including the role of law enforcement in creating strong and trusting partnerships with the community. The workshop also provided a platform for community members to analyze and vet law enforcement practices from the community's perspective (PDX 2015)."*

Community member, Kimberly Dixon from the Center of Intercultural Organizing stated, *"I gained a great respect for the participants in this training in being part of the process of real and positive efforts that bridge the civil service work of law enforcement and community. Efforts such as this from all involved give hope to the intentionality of building greatness in our respective cities (PDX 2015)."* Approximately 100 chiefs, captains and lieutenants from across the state of

Oregon attended along with 60 diverse community members. The overall consensus from all participants: community members and local police need more facilitated opportunities to interact, learn, listen, share and build with one other. Those who are policing well, know that community engagement and cultivating trust is the foundation to creating public safety.

The Columbian newspaper in Vancouver, Washington featured T4T's Diversity Team in an article entitled, "Vancouver PD Strives for Diversity, not Animosity." *"Instead of trying to eliminate all bias in law enforcement, we encourage departments to discover the humanity and struggle within various demographics living in their respective jurisdictions,"* Lee said. Chief David Henslee of the Klamath Falls Police Department stated, *"I was pleased with the open engagement and personal interaction between law enforcement and community members. The training provided an opportunity for participants to have honest and meaningful dialogue about issues that impact human interactions."*

The transformation of relationships, organizations and society requires a deep commitment to justice, healing and community building. It is emotionally challenging, time consuming and not a one size fits all module. Transformation requires authentic opportunities to engage, listen, share and be heard. The work that we do and the timing that we have done it is truly unique. We have spent countless hours over the last two decades researching and understanding law enforcement agencies and their responses to police killings, police misconduct and racial profiling. Further, we have dug deep to retain curriculum, trainers, modules and consultants they hire to improve upon their practices.

What is missing and needed:
1. Allocate funding opportunities for law enforcement and community members to build trust and transform relationships in a safe environment with highly trained facilitators
2. Law Enforcement agencies begin tracking excessive force incidents and making public all data collected related to vehicles, bicyclists and pedestrian stops https://data.cityofberkeley.info/
3. License T4T's **21st Century Conscious Based Leadership Curriculum** in LEO training nationwide
4. License **Community Conscious Policing Curriculum** to law enforcement agencies nationwide
5. Mandate Continuing Education in Law Enforcement focused on Equity and Community Building
6. Partner with educational institutions related to social justice and transformative learning
7. Establish AND Fund Citizen Oversight of Police & Accountability Boards
   - National Association for Civilian Oversight of Law Enforcement (NACOLE)

Police Accountability and Reform

According to the New World of Police Accountability written by Samuel Walker and Carol Archbold, second edition, there have been great strides worth noting in regard to community policing efforts nationwide. Throughout the past fifty years, several important measures in police reform include, but are not excluded to (Walker 2014):

1. Supreme Court decisions (Mapp v. Ohio, Miranda v. Arizona, Rodriguez v. United States)
2. Birth and spread of **community policing** and problem-oriented policing
3. New restrictions on police use of deadly force, high speed pursuits
4. Growth of significant representation of African American, Latino and female police officers
5. The spread of **citizen oversight** of the police
6. Improvements in police officer educational levels and **training** programs
7. Increased awareness for the need of highly skilled and effective mental health response

On a local level, the City of Dallas Police Department implemented an eight point plan that represents *"a pursuit in police accountability at its best* (Walker 2014)." If all law enforcement agencies acted as **quickly** and **proactively** to controversial incidents, the need for litigation would greatly be reduced. In 2012, Dallas experienced a series of officer involved shootings. One in particular on July 24th, included an unarmed resident who was killed by police. As a result, the community protested and demanded accountability reform. Within two weeks, the chief issued the Eight Point Plan for New Policies and Strategic Directives, which included the following (Walker 2014):

1. Formalizing a relationship with the Federal Bureau of Investigation for concurrent investigations into all officer-involved shootings
2. A more comprehensive policy for officers reporting resistance to officer incidents
3. Revising the foot pursuit policy to reduce risks to officers and preventing escalating use of force
4. **Research Best Practices** from around the nation
5. **Proactive Response** to an immediate community controversy
6. Reform went beyond officer involved shootings to **include other issues related to equity**
7. Recognized that <u>fatal shootings of unarmed people</u> are OFTEN the result of **failures in Policies, Training** and **Supervision**.

Also in 2012, the U.S. Justice Department published a Collaborative Report on use of force by the Las Vegas Metropolitan Police over officer-involved shootings. It represents a promising **middle ground** between proactive community policing efforts and mandated police reform. The report represented a **joint effort** between a new Critical Response Technical Assistance Program in the United States Department of Justice, a private consulting firm like Training 4 Transformation, LLC, and the local police department. The recommended changes included (Walker 2014):

1. VMPD's use of force policy, which included *"a mission statement that emphasizes the sanctity of human life"*
2. An emphasis on de-escalating officer-citizen encounters
3. Tighter restrictions on conducted energy devices (taser, firearms, K9, vehicle and pedestrian pursuits)
4. **A broader view of shooting incidents to include community perspective**
5. **Improvements in consistency, quality and quantity of training on various issues**
6. Detailed work plan for a continuing collaborative process through which the COPS Office **[and private firm with an equity lens]** would assist in implementing recommendations, including a set of goals and timetables, with the cooperation of the law enforcement agency

Through the **consent decree** between the U.S. Justice Department and New Orleans Police Department, it mandated sweeping accountability-related reforms throughout the institution. Similar to fifteen other consent decrees throughout the nation, New Orleans included (Walker 2014):

1. Improving the department's use of CED devices (including vehicle pursuits, use of K9 units, taser, firearms)
2. Development of a crisis intervention team for handling mental health cases

3. New policies governing stops, searches, arrests and custodial interrogation

Consent Decrees tend to result from settlements between the U.S. Justice Department and local or state law enforcement agencies regarding a *"pattern or practice"* of violations of the constitutional rights of people. In New Orleans, the decree went a step beyond previous settlement agreements in two meaningful ways (Walker 2014):

1. It included a section devoted to **GENDER BIAS**. The report required new police policies related to the investigation of sexual assault cases and the handling of domestic violence incidents.

2. It included **formal requirements designed to ensure greater community input** into the implementation of the consent decree and into the police department once the decree was eventually lifted.

The consent decree in New Orleans represents what should be the **last resort** when it comes to police accountability, which is a lawsuit by the U.S. Justice Department mandating sweeping reforms. In most cases, a department embedded with inequity is not capable of institutional corrective action on its own. *"The reports of independent court-appointed monitors in several cases found that the departments had been transformed in a positive direction (Walker 2014)."* For example, the monitor for the New Jersey State Police consent decree concluded in its final report that the agency had become **self-monitoring** and

self-correcting *"to a degree not often observed in American law enforcement* (Walker 2014)."

The monitor for the Washington D.C. Police Department reached a similarly optimistic conclusion in its final report. However, sustaining reforms in all areas of policing is a major challenge. At a conference in 2012 on Federal Pattern or Practice sponsored by the Police Executive Research Forum, several police chiefs who had been through the consent decree experience explained how it had improved their departments in the end (Walker 2014):

1. Reduction in violence – shootings had dropped by 80% and have since remained low
2. Reduction in civil suit damages by tens, maybe even hundreds, of thousands of dollars from years prior
3. Gave the police department credibility with the public

What sets the Dallas Eight Point Plan apart from other efforts is the way in which the chief proactively addressed officer-involved shootings and other issues. *"In the new police accountability, police departments will* **respond proactively, become self-monitoring** *and* **develop into learning organizations** *where* <u>*they seek to learn from problems and mistakes that occur and develop appropriate corrective responses*</u> (Walker 2014)." Many police departments, maybe even most, are not in a position to conduct a thorough **self-study or equity evaluation** of their existing policies that include hiring practices, budget allocation and a thorough understanding of the cultural dynamics for the residents they serve .

A genuine commitment to community conscious policing strategies involves an organizational culture of accountability, which includes the following procedures (Walker 2014):

1. An **early intervention system** and how it can be used to its fullest potential to reduce violence, liabilities and restore trust with the community
2. **Assistance from outside experts** is a valuable and even a necessary process
3. Consult an outside expert, such as Training 4 Transformation, LLC, who will **identify existing or potential problems and recommend corrective action**

SECTION I

Data Collection

Context

According to the United States Census Bureau of 2010, Oregon residents comprise of the following:

(a) = Portland (b) = Oregon

- White alone 2010 (a) 76.1% – Portland (b) 83.6% – Oregon
- Black or African American alone, 2010 (a) 6.3% (b) 1.8%
- American Indian and Alaska Native alone, 2010 (a) 1.0% ((b) 1.4%
- Asian alone, 2010 (a) 7.1% (b) 3.7%
- Native Hawaiian and Other Pacific Islander alone, 2010 (a) 0.5% (b) 0.3%
- Two or More Races 2010 (a) 4.7% (b) 3.8%
- Hispanic or Latino 2010 (a) 9.4% (b) 11.7%
- Foreign born persons 2009-2013 (a) 13.8% (b) 9.8%
- Language other than English spoken at home, pct age 5+, 2009-2013 (a) 18.9% (b) 14.8%
- Persons below poverty level 2009-2013 (a) 17.8% (b) 16.2%

Business QuickFacts
- Black-owned firms 2007 (a) 3.1% – Portland (b) 1.2% – Oregon
- American Indian- and Alaska Native-owned firms 2007 (a) 0.8% (b) 1.2%
- Asian-owned firms 2007 (a) 6.7% (b) 3.6%
- Native Hawaiian and Other Pacific Islander-owned firms 2007 (a) 0.2% (b) 0.2%
- Hispanic-owned firms 2007 (a) 3.0% (b) 3.3%

In 2011, the Oregon Law Enforcement Contacts Committee (LECC) joined the Criminal Justice Policy Research Institute (CJPRI) at Portland State University and the Salem Oregon Police (SPD) to publish a report on critical issues in law enforcement entitled "Decreasing Crime by Increasing Involvement: A Guidebook for Building Relations in Multi-Ethnic Communities." It begins with a racial breakdown of Oregon underserved residents:

Oregon Office of Economic Analysis
- 11.7% of Oregonians Hispanic or Latino
- 21.5% of Oregonians belonged to an underrepresented ethnic group or race

Pew Hispanic Center
- lists Oregon and Washington as two of seven states with the largest Latino population growth; with each having a more than 130% increase in the last decade

The Coalition of Communities of Color
- 9th largest urban Native American population in the United States resides in Multnomah County

Immigrant Refugee and Community Organization
- Oregon is the 11th largest refugee recipient state in the nation, taking in approximately 1,200 refugees every year
- Somali Community Services Coalition of Oregon estimates that the Somali population within the state

of Oregon has grown to approximately 8,000 and that approximately 2,500 have moved to Oregon within the last two years (2009 - 2011)

A Systemic Problem

The Decreasing Crime by Increasing Involvement report also highlights the role of past Oregon Race Exclusion Laws as a context for understanding the current dynamics of police-community relations throughout the state. For example, in 1844 slavery was prohibited by Oregon's Provisional Government; however, the government also enacted measures forcing Blacks to leave the state or be whipped twice a year. In 1850, up to 320 free acres were granted to white males. The same enactment prohibited blacks from being granted acreage (CJPRI 2011).

Additionally, while the U.S. government was implementing laws of equality into the U.S. Constitution, such as the 14th Amendment in 1868 (granting citizenship by birth and ensuring due process) and the 15th Amendment in 1870 (providing all citizens the right to vote), Oregon's legislature refused to incorporate or support this progress towards equal rights (CJPRI 2011). In both 1919 and 1923, Laws and business practices were created to restrict and in some cases prevent people of color from purchasing property. For first generation Japanese Americans, they were also prevented from owning land due to the Alien Land Law (CJPRI 2011).

According to the Los Angeles Times, Oregon offers a good example of how a racist statute can end up staying on the books:

"A constitutional provision dating from 1857 states that 'No free negro, or mulatto, not residing in this State at the time of the adoption of this Constitution, shall come, reside, or be within this State, or hold any real estate ....'

Another provision facing removal states the number of Oregon Supreme Court justices 'shall not exceed five until the white population of the State shall amount to One Hundred Thousand.'

Many early settlers were pro-slavery Democrats, Southerners who brought with them their social norms, and sometimes their slaves.

In 1868, the U.S. Congress ratified the 14th Amendment, which bars states from enforcing laws that deny citizens equal protection based on race. Oregon voters in 1925 repealed their state's constitutional provisions discriminating against blacks. But the language — forgotten by many and ignored by others — was never removed

*State Sen. Avel Gordly (D-Portland) prodded lawmakers in the **2001 legislative session** to prepare Measure 14, which <u>would finally remove the obsolete language</u> (Prengaman 2002)."*

As a result of biased legislation from 1844 – 1959, opportunity gaps widened between affluent white residents and minority Oregonians. The impact on underserved communities are still prevelant today and is well documented in the Oregon Education Investment Board Equity Lens (2013). For example, gentrification, police excessive force against residents impacted by mental health, undocumented, rural, houseless, formerly incarcerated, foster care students, transgendered, multi-ethnic, bi-racial, English language learners, Muslim, Refugees and Immigrants are the types of community members we specialize in connecting directly with decision makers of local law enforcement. Training For Transformation, LLC endorses the LECC report, "Decreasing Crime by Increasing Involvement: A Guidebook for Building Relations in Multi-Ethnic Communities (2011)" as a step in the right direction toward Community Conscious policing efforts. However, the optimal way to increase involvement by community in law enforcement is to hire and promote them.

SB 560: End of Racial Profiling Bill

"In 1994, the Oregon Supreme Court performed a system-wide audit of racial bias in the administration of justice in Oregon and confirmed that people of color are more likely to be arrested, charged, convicted and incarcerated and less likely to be released on bails or put on probation (CIO 2006)."

In 2015, the Oregon State Legislature passed SB 560, *"the End Racial Profiling Bill. It would ban racial profiling tied to personal descriptions or circumstances, except in cases where law enforcement has received information tied to a specific case."* The bill would require all law enforcement agencies to take steps to eliminate profiling and the Attorney General is charged to create an independent complaints procedure to investigate racial profiling complaints (CIO 2006).

The partnership who introduced the bill to state representatives include the Center for Intercultural Organizing,

Northwest Constitutional Rights Center, Portland Police Bureau, American Civil Liberties Union and Northwest Federation of Community Organizations. In order to glean insights from community members directly, the partnership hosted Listening Sessions where police and community convened to hear about the impacts of racial profiling (CIO 2006).

Community and Police Listening Sessions Report

The Listening Sessions Report: A Community and Police Partnership to Eliminate Racial Profiling in 2006 determined, *"The city government's (Portland) current system for complaints of racial profiling by police is ineffective. This allowed listening session organizers to establish a constructive, collaborative environment in which both community members and police were actively engaged in dialogue with one another and in finding solutions to racial profiling together (CIO 2006)."* As a result of listening sessions and other public forums where community engaged with local police and public officials, Portland Mayor Hales established the Community Peace Collaborative with the Portland Police Bureau where residents and community continued working together toward peaceful resolutions.

Appendix D of the Listening Session Report (2006):

> *"Lt. Dana Lewis, training officer for the Portland Police Bureau, conducted the Perspectives in Profiling training in July 2006 for members of the Listening Sessions Planning Committee so they could experience and evaluate the training program first hand. All*

sworn officers within the Portland Police Bureau completed this course as part of their 2006 in-service training. According to Lt. Lewis, the training was developed as an eight hour program, but it was reduced to only three hours to accommodate the limited training time officers have. Perspectives in Profiling is a video role-playing training program that presents officers with ethical dilemmas. Their path through the training program is determined by the decisions that they make. While all listening sessions committee members thought the training was a good first step, segments of the training left participants skeptical that officers would respond as the video enactments suggested.

Participants were also concerned that an in-service program designed to take eight hours had been cut to three, eliminating potentially good information and context from the training. Additionally, **a multi-ethnic training team would strengthen the training program. Unfortunately, most Portland Police Bureau training seminars lack multi-ethnic training staff. The committee believes the participation of people of color in PPB diversity and cultural competency training is essential to develop better understanding of varying cultural and ethnic norms that can impede effective and respectful communication.**

While video enactments have their place in training rapid decision-making, **active participation by the community in preparing officers for their** *__work__ will not only demonstrate community support of the Portland Police Bureau, but __will better prepare new officers for the experiences they will encounter as they are learning to be culturally-competent community policing professionals__. Additionally, __bringing the community into the process of training officers creates a shared set of expectations of how the officers will respond when they are in the local community.__"*

As a result, Training 4 Transformation has incorporated the recommendations from the Community Listening Sessions and Decreasing Crime by Increasing Involvement Reports, in addition to suggestions made by other credible sources like the United States Department of Justice Community Oriented Policing Services (COPS). Not to mention, feedback from thousands of diverse Oregon residents.

Key to Successful Community Policing

According to What Works in Community Policing published by Berkeley Law (2013), the following strategies were identified to assist police departments engage in effective community policing efforts:

1. Form community partnerships with a wide-range of partners, above and beyond active resident groups

2. __Increase the department's accessibility to the residents it serves__

3. **Train personnel at every level of the department in best practices in community policing**

4. Work towards increasing officer buy-in about the benefits of the community policing philosophy

5. Prioritize sustained and meaningful commitment by the department's leadership to the community policing philosophy

6. **Integrate community policing activities into performance evaluation systems**

7. Continue to support systematic and standardized problem solving approaches

SECTION II

Who are we?

T4T Overview

Training for Transformation, LLC (T4T) is a minority, women, emerging small business owned certified firm that works with public agencies to support them in creating a culture of equity and inclusion. Depending on the needs of the agency, T4T offers a range of services necessary for organizations to culturally shift. This process includes conducting equity evaluations and assessments, coaching leaders and management through systemic transitions, building employees and stakeholders trust, increasing employee's cultural competency and confidence, establishing systems of accountability and creating sustainable equitable systems.

Our services are implemented collaboratively, thoughtfully and tailored for the specific needs and environments of each agency using experiential learning models and informed by the industry's best and next practices. In the short time that T4T has been established, we have worked with the City of Corvallis Police Department, FBI National Academy Associates (FBINAA), City of Portland Parks & Recreation, Portland Community College, teachers, students, advocates, community and non-profit organizations.

Training 4 Transformation's Law Enforcement Community Building Workshops based on experiential learning and equity-focused facilitation have transcended traditional barriers. Our trainers are certified in conflict transformation, multilingual, lived or worked internationally while maintaining roots locally. More importantly, what has emerged is an innovative co-creative process that we coined *Community Conscious Policing* after developing curriculum alongside the City of Corvallis Police Department, FBI National Academy Association and hundreds of community participants.

Founders

Hun Taing, co-founder and CEO of Training for Transformation, LLC has over fifteen years experience transforming communities, organizations and institutions. She is a Cambodian refugee who grew up in Long Beach, California, lived internationally and worked on both coasts of the U.S. with an acumen for cross cultural awareness, equity and inclusion that cuts through language, cultural and religious barriers. She has a long history organizing and empowering immigrants and refugees to advocate for economic justice, immigrant rights and civil rights. She's a systems' thinker, strategic and practical with the ability to open hearts and the skills to mobilize and inspire people to take action. Hun earned a BA in Sociology from the University of California, Santa Barbara and a MA in Conflict Transformation from the School for International Training Graduate Institute.

Brandon J. Lee, co-founder and President of Training for Transformation, LLC is a proud Black man born and raised in Oakland, California. With a lifetime of experience personally advocating for justice against profiling and institutional racism, he has become the expert in transforming traumatic circumstances into a hopeful victorious one. His understanding of how to correct and restore institutions to a healthy and inclusive environment is unmatched. Brandon is a regular presenter and speaker at colleges, universities and conferences on topics that include: Black Founding Fathers of the U.S., Community Conscious Policing, Black Male Achievement, English as a Second Language and 21st Century Leadership. Fluent in Spanish, Brandon has lived, studied and taught in Spain, Cuba and Mexico. He has taught English as a Second Language for five years at universities both domestic and abroad to international students from around the world and brings a globally minded lens to locally focused situations. Brandon earned a BA in Public Policy and Spanish from Houston Baptist University and a MA in Teaching from the School for International Training Graduate Institute.

T4T Approach

T4T specializes in community conscious policing strategies by confronting bias, prejudice, discrimination, privilege and oppression through a co-creative experiential learning process. The answers community and law enforcement seek for their respective issues can be found in a transparent and co-creative structure which allows for all members of the area served to provide solutions to the prevalent issues in a specific community. We invite law enforcement to reach out to members of the general population, being careful not to focus solely on community, political and religious leaders. We focus outreach efforts on the general population to gain community access and personally invite the constituents who are often excluded from society so their voices can be integrated into process.

Our focus is with law enforcement agencies who are ready for more than the module training and ready for a deeper and more authentic community building.

Community Conscious Policing Workshop

Community Conscious Policing is a concept we coined to describe a culturally competent, equitable and empathetic approach to law enforcement that is inclusive of all underserved community or vulnerable populations in a co-creative educational process that benefits law enforcement and the commnities they serve.

Training For Transformation workshops are multi-faceted and dynamic using diverse formats and experiential learning that maximize engagement, sharing and learning. Together, we explore how cultural and racial stereotypes influence our beliefs and its impact on communities. Additionally, the workshop aims to increase awareness about the roles and responsibilities of law enforcement personnel in creating strong and trusting partnerships within the community, and how those partnerships can benefit neighborhood residents.

Workshop Objectives

- To engage in authentic and meaningful exchanges that will build rapport and increase understanding between community members and officers

- To identify and challenge stereotypes, assumptions and prejudices regarding specific community groups and police officers

- To humanize the experiences of community groups and police officers

- To identify concrete outcomes that will further relationship building between agencies and its community members

Fred Edwards, CEO Knight Vision Security

SECTION III

What do we do?

City of Corvallis Police Department
<u>Community Building Workshop</u>

NAACP Corvallis Branch Meeting with City of Corvallis PD Leadership

As the Legal Redress Committee Chairman for the NAACP Corvallis branch at the time, I received dozens of discrimination complaints and racial profiling cases regarding law enforcement from community members in Corvallis, Lebanon, Albany, Salem and Portland. My role was to work with the affected members to educate, empower and correct the wrong by facilitating communication between parties.

One day at an NAACP Corvallis branch meeting, Chief Jon Sassaman, in his community outreach efforts came to speak. We were impressed with the data he presented that indicated little or no police misconduct or racial profiling in recent years. However, statistics do not always capture all of our experiences. More importantly, the chief came to learn how his department was doing from a community perspective.

Once we expressed interest in working in partnership with the Corvallis Police Department, Lieutenant Jim Zessin contacted me for a meeting. He arrived at my office in plain clothes. This disarmed me, because I was expecting a "big bad" cop like the ones who had harassed me growing up in Oakland. We sat down to talk, and he opened up first about his experiences as a minority in the marines. Then he shared his vision of equity in law enforcement, elaborated on the chief's investment into training and education for his leadership, and the ways in which officers should be held accountable when boundaries are crossed. Lieutenant Zessin took a personal interest in me inquiring about my childhood and family.

We followed up with our first meeting where, Hun and I met with Training Lieutenant Jim Zessin, Police Union President and Sergeant Michael Mann along with Police Instructor, Officer Nick Hurley. Upon arriving to the City of Corvallis Police Department, we were greeted by Jim who gave us a thorough tour of the facilities. He showed us every room where evidence is stored, how it is checked in, the checks and balances to ensure it was secure, where officers train and introduced us to every officer and staff on duty. He was transparent on where they had hoped to improve and where they had made great strides. Our first order of business was to get to know one another.

I shared my numerous experiences of being racially profiled by law enforcement in every city that I have lived in including Oakland, Berkeley and San Diego, California, Newark, Delaware and Waco, Texas. I talked about the generations of Black men in my family being harassed and profiled by law enforcement and the impact it had on me, the family and mothers in my family. The officers shared their experiences with diversity, challenges of being a police officer, what they enjoyed most about their jobs and their inspiration for becoming a police officer. For us, it was the first time we got to know officers beyond their badge. For example, one officer had grown up in rural Oregon and had never met a Black person until attending college. He did not grow up racist; but rather, he hadn't met anyone who looked or lived differently until leaving home. It didn't diminish his enthusiasm to embed equity in policy, staff and budgetary decisions. In fact, he went out of his way to value diversity and supported our collaboration wholeheartedly.

City of Corvallis Police Chief Jon Sassaman

Collectively, CPD and T4T wanted to duplicate and recreate this experience of validation and humanization that I personally did not believe was possible before. We were determined to recreate this opportunity for others with the goal of *"humanizing our respective experiences and to bring people together who might otherwise remain at a perpetual distance."*

Process

My first impression of CPD leadership was they were extremely educated, not only about police tactics, but also 21st century leadership practices centered on empathy, compassion and consciousness. This way of processing is based on right brain cognition (Pink 2005) and has evolved into conscious based leadership where survival is based on the wisest rather than the strongest. A working definition of Conscious Based Leadership is, *"the art of leading one's self to be in tune with natural law."*

During the Jim Crow era of segregation and even slavery, linear models of policing where officers simply escalate one level beyond a suspect to maintain control of a situation is nearly counter-productive nowadays.

This approach is based on left brain processing (Pink 2005) that is simply outdated, which has led to thousands of unarmed people of color, mentally challenged, women, transgendered, undocumented residents and houseless community members being unnecessarily killed by law enforcement nationwide. Our first step as a team was to learn more about CPD and how they trained their officers around inclusion. They admitted that their agency was comprised of mostly White men; however, they wanted our input on recruiting, retention and training from a community lens.

Second, we evaluated their Museum of Tolerance Diversity Training manual. CPD had sent their training lieutenant to Los Angeles, CA to be trained in the curriculum so he could implement it back in Oregon. That in itself demonstrated an institutional level of support for diversity and inclusion efforts. For weeks, Hun and I reviewed the manuals, videos and training resources CPD provided us in good faith. We were careful not to violate their trust, so we kept its contents confidential. Our biggest critique was that the curriculum relied too much on outdated simulated scenarios versus real life community engagement, and it did not require officers to purge themselves of implicit bias.

For example, the curriculum promoted virtues that are necessary to be effective while on duty but it did not provide officers with the tools to confront internalized bias, privilege and oppression. The training video regarding excessive force used real life dash cam footage from patrol cars that were decades old. In addition, officers trained for the worst-case scenario in nearly every engagement with community. I understand that their life is at stake; but as a survivor of police misconduct, my safety and civil rights as a community member is just as important to protect.

Finally, when we delivered our feedback to CPD, the nation had erupted into a polarized dialogue after an unarmed Black teen was killed by a police officer in Ferguson, Missouri. The protests resulted in a state of emergency and the nation sat nervously awaiting to hear if officer Darrin Wilson would be tried for murder. As tensions on campus rose for students, Hun and I decided we needed to do something. With my teacher trainer experience and her expertise in conflict transformation, we researched police training methods since every officer involved in a shooting says they were simply *"following training protocol."* Through our research, we also found the U.S. Department of Justice would mandate training to help departments, like Ferguson, close systemic gaps.

After further investigation, Hun and I discovered that there was no training available where law enforcement could engage directly with the community they serve through a professionally facilitated, equity-focused dialogue like T4T. We found diversity trainings, but nearly all of them preached to police in a vacuum without providing tools and support necessary to engage real people in the neighborhood. For example, tensions remained high due to the trend of unarmed Black men being killed by police nationwide. As a former English as a Second Language collegiate faculty member, I am reminded of an increasing number of international students and refugees who would engage local police for a variety of reasons.

At a local community college, I saw firsthand how campus police received little to no training on how to engage with minority demographics like transgendered, formerly incarcerated, undocumented and international students. Their lack of cultural competence and training often translated into some form of trauma for students, faculty and staff particularly if these officers are armed. Ultimately, the institution is left responsible for their actions. We at T4T firmly believe that arming police on school grounds and college campuses is **not** the answer. Community building is our response to buying a gun.

T4T's only option was to recruit local community members along with the police department and train them together through community conscious policing experiential learning exercises. Officers would have the opportunity to learn directly from the community they serve. In exchange, community would learn more about the challenges that officers face, how to engage with law enforcement and hold rogue officers accountable who cross the boundary. Our collective goal was to provide a safe space to heal, share experiences and build a collective vision for what community conscious policing means to all stakeholders.

Amidst protests and a state of emergency declared in Ferguson, Missouri after unarmed Michael Brown was killed by Officer Darrin Wilson, T4T was inviting community to engage directly with police. While the polarization of law enforcement and communities of color were widening, we were working against the grain to close the gap. During a time when it was not popular to be friendly nor to be working with law enforcement, we were taking that risk and pressure to do something proactive.

Ferguson burning: A demonstrator sits in front of a street fire during a Ferguson demonstration in Oakland, California.
Photo: Reuters (Photo: Charlie Riedel, AP)

Context

In 2012, I served as a faculty member and administrator in student affairs at Oregon State University where my department supported over four hundred student led clubs, multicultural and international student-led organizations. In the women's center on campus, a violent hate letter was found in a suggestion box in the women's restroom one week prior to winter term finals. The letter was directed at the only African women who worked in the women's center, and it threatened violence against her and other Black students.

As an administrator, I served on the bias response team that was going to be addressing this matter. I assumed that the team would be working with students, staff and law enforcement to solve this case and make the student whole. Instead, a group of executive level administrators put forth every effort to protect the university at the expense of the survivor. As a result, the crime was never solved nor reported as a hate crime. The victim, who also was a United States citizen, was denied access to academic scholarships that she had earned, threatened to lose financial aid and worst of all, blamed for writing the hate letter found in the women's center. In response, I continued my career in community and educational advocacy here in Oregon.

Oregon State University Hate Letter
—Women's Center 2014

Hello WC Staff,

I think that Black people belong on the noose. They need to be killed and lynched like old times so that they know their place. I do not know why you have a black person in your midlst, it is completely ridiculous that we are mixing races. I do not know how a black person can be a feminist or even call themselves educated. She belongs on the nose and should be lynched so that she knows who she is or where she comes from. We are letting black people invade our space and she dares support her director and GTA as if she mattered or even existed. She does not know that she is invisible; that she is fucking black and does not have a place here among the educated people at OSU. She better watch her back or she will end up on the noose. Again I believe that she would be lynched, black people are fucking stupid; those niggers don't belong among us; or at the Women center

First Lady of the United States of America Michelle Obama

Community Building

The first step was to assess the survivor's peers through an anonymous survey to discover if others had also been the victim of hate crimes on campus as well. For legal redress purposes, the surveys would determine if this hate crime was an isolated incident or indeed a pattern of systemic bias that had simply been ignored by police and administration? The feedback we received was overwhelming. We were able to establish a consistent pattern of racial profiling on or near campus by not only fellow students but also faculty, administrators and patrol officers.

Unfortunately, many of the students did not recall which law enforcement agencies had profiled or harassed them. This indicated to me that there needs to be legal redress training for community, so they know what information is most pertinent when filing a formal complaint after their civil liberties have been violated. For this reason, T4T has partnered with the Law Enforcement Coordinating Committee (LECC) to provide this valuable information to community who tend to be most underserved.

In regard to the hate crime on campus, our branch of the NAACP could not determine based on the data collected what law enforcement agencies had allegedly racially profiled the students. There are five different agencies in the same city, whose headquarters are in the same building. Was it the Department of Public Safety on campus, local police department or the sheriff's office? Therefore, I was unable to hold a law enforcement agency accountable for the racial profiling alleged in the student surveys.

The good that came from all of our collective efforts is that I followed the U.S. Department of Justice recommendation and contacted Chief Sassaman of our local police department who I had previously met at our branch meeting. The chief had attended to connect directly with the community and to open dialogue. He came prepared with data his department had collected regarding traffic stops and could statistically determine that racial bias was not present in his patrol. However, I wanted to see what we both could glean from the qualitative data I had collected from students as educators and law enforcement. It was our collective duty to ensure the safety of our students while on or near campus.

Humanizing our Collective Experiences

Regarding the survivor from the women's center, my wife and I worked tirelessly to connect her with trauma support from a culturally specific counselor, advocated for her financial aid to be reinstated and by the end of Spring term 2014, she had earned over $20,000 in academic scholarships! She will graduate soon as one of only three Black women in her cohort. Most importantly, through the community building workshop, she was able to build alliances with CPD leadership, patrol officers and even build some camaraderie with many of the female officers. For example, wearing her Muslim hijab made the survivor feel like a target on the bus around town. As a result, she would walk for miles to avoid riding public transportation.

After she moved to more affordable housing off campus, she felt compelled to remove her traditional dress in order to safely get to and from school without feeling isolated or being harassed. Out of everyone in the room, the person who most identified with her story of being a targeted African, Muslim woman in rural Oregon was a white middle aged woman who worked on parking patrol. The stories she told of how she was mistreated while on duty giving tickets to vehicles who are parked illegally made many of us understand the harassment that some police feel too. Even though the officer owned a gun and could certainly protect herself if needed, these two people from very different backgrounds found a common ground where they could empower one another simply by sharing their respective stories in a safe space. By working with local law enforcement, we as educators were able to ensure a safe environment for underserved students that translated into increased retention.

Challenges

1. **We did not know if current events and media attention would help or hinder our efforts to build bridges for community and law enforcement?**

This idea of a Community Building Workshop with Law Enforcement was frankly crazy, especially as other cases of police shootings of other unarmed Black men began to take over national media attention. Eric Gardner in New York was choked to death on camera by NYPD for allegedly selling loose cigarettes, a minor misdemeanor offense. A 12 -year old named Tamir was killed in the park while playing with a toy gun. Another Black male teen was killed while shopping in a store, holding a toy gun and talking on the cell phone. In South Carolina, a Black man was killed by an officer on camera who also was recorded planting evidence on the scene to support his bogus claims of feeling like his life was in danger. On camera, it is obvious the driver ran away in the opposite direction as he was being shot repeatedly by the officer. Each incident had been recorded using cell phone video recorders, highlighting biased policing practices nation-wide and none of the departments had a training experience focused on equity quite like T4T.

2. How do we recruit 50 – 70 community members to attend our Community Building Workshop?

New Recruits with the City of Corvallis PD

It was important that we did NOT focus solely on inviting community "representatives or leaders." What cities often discover during times of crisis is that those who are recognized to be "community leaders," typically are not. Maybe they had been at one time. However, nowadays, there is a trend of people put in place for a salary, to qualify for government funding or to ensure that no true progress is made for underserved communities on a systemic level. Individual successes do not make up for collective failures of institutions to adequately serve everyone equitably, not just equally.

T4T focuses our energy on providing access for those residents whose voice is rarely integrated into the dialogue or process so they could be heard directly by decision makers. For example, members from the Mental Health, LGBTQ, communities in recovery, single mothers, foster children, immigrants, disabled and the houseless communities were a few of the underserved communities we focused our efforts on attending. We would train the entire City of Corvallis Police Department including dispatch, administration staff and parking enforcement on how to engage more consciously. Therefore, the challenge I was most concerned about was recruiting enough participants and then having them evenly dispersed throughout the four workshops. The first being during the day on a Tuesday and the second scheduled on a Friday. Recruiting for Tuesday while community had to work would be my first challenge to overcome.

Due to our professional and civic engagement, my wife and I were able to utilize our personal networks in supporting our outreach efforts. Specifically, being an officer in both NAACP and the local Freemason lodge helped me to save money and find support recruiting. Ultimately, we recruited nearly seventy community members to attend all four workshops. Even the chief attended, which made an incredible impression on everyone especially me. To provide a safe space, we agreed to lead four workshops over two days in order to reduce each group size under fifty people. Since the officers were compensated and mandated to attend by Chief Sassaman, it was evident that he was committed to our workshops and took an incredible risk to remain on the cutting edge of law enforcement practices.

3. The workshops were held during the week between office hours. **How could we convince community members to take off from work, find a way to the workshop and then engage with the local police department for free?**

We resorted to the original organizing model of Each 1, Reach 1 then Teach 1. In other words, Hun and I mapped out everyone from our personal and professional networks that had a vested interest in this project for a variety of reasons. Then we recruited and asked them to find another who fit the same criteria. It was important that we did not utilize any social media or public outlets for outreach as we did not want our event mistaken for many other gimmicks. Therefore, it took roughly 3 months to recruit over a hundred community members and 70 actually attended.

4. **How could we as a consulting agency ensure all participants safety?** On the news everyday during this time were protests against police nationwide and a state of emergency in Ferguson, MO. There were officers terrified of actually sitting in the same room for hours or even having to talk to someone they had arrested in the past. **How could we moderate and mediate touchy situations as they arose?**

Actually, we did have a participant attempt to call out a specific officer who he felt had unjustly arrested him in the past. Personally, I had delivered ground rules to the group and this was a clear violation. To preserve the harmony of the workshop, it was imperative that I remind the group of the ground rules and move on without inviting the person back into the dialogue. Although he shared his grievances with me on his evaluation later that afternoon, the officers present appreciated that Hun and I had the skills to keep everyone focused through guided experiential learning exercises that reduced opportunities like these to disrupt our primary goal, which was to build community.

In order to gain some familiarity with the community we recruited, our team chose to implement an application to attend since seats were limited. The first round of applications, we included basic demographic information but also the objectives and overview of the workshops to set clear expectations. Once we collected all of the applications, I called each participant personally and explained that we would administer a background check with their consent. The purpose was to ensure safety for everyone attending. What we needed to make clear was that we were not excluding applicants with a criminal history. We specifically were concerned with anyone who had an open case pending with Corvallis PD or anyone who had been arrested for assaulting or evading a police officer. We wanted officers to know we had taken every precaution to ensure our workshop would be a safe event where they did not have to worry about securing the premises.

5.   **Where do we host the Community Building Workshop with CPD and NAACP?**

Once we had applications for community recruitment and background checks administered, we had to decide on a location that would be conducive for providing a safe space and ethos for everyone. When I first moved to Corvallis, I transferred my membership to Corvallis #14 which is the Freemason lodge in town. Historically, it was founded in 1859 which happens to be the year Oregon was established and also the year the Oregon Exclusion Laws prohibited people of color from moving or staying in the state.

Over the course of one hundred and fifty years, the laws were repealed by the Portland NAACP branch. Since aspects of our Community Building Workshop with local law enforcement included addressing systemic and institutional bias, we felt it imperative to host it in the oldest building in the city. I was the first Black member to join Corvallis #14 in over 150 years (that I am aware of) and now it would become the host for reconciliation for all neighbors in town. This was the original purpose of why I joined the lodge, which is *"to bring those together who may otherwise remain at a perpetual distance."*

Triumphs

The triumphs were too numerous to count. For example, officers felt comfortable sharing about losing their partner in the line of duty. Community participants got to hear about the stresses of police being overworked, the challenges of being available for family outside of work, not being able to go out in public without having to always be in police mode and learning directly from officers how to engage with them in an optimal way. Community participants got to know local patrol and parking enforcement on a first name basis and connect with them through shared experiences revealed throughout the day. In addition, colleagues with CPD learned more about one another, although many of them had worked together for years.

Above all, Corvallis police officers were able to learn more about the complexity of the constituents they serve. For example, defining the differences and overlap between international students, refugees, immigrants,

migrants and undocumented community members proved to be necessary. CPD learned how many community members share similar feelings for different reasons. For example, as a Black man growing up in Oakland, I will always be triggered anytime a police car gets behind my vehicle. A parking enforcement attendant who works with law enforcement also feared getting pulled over, but not because she was Black or from Oakland. As a single mother, one ticket could prevent her from being able to provide her kids with a birthday party or Christmas presents. Everyday, she lives with this fear of some unexpected event happening and not being able to provide for her family.

We had a self identified lesbian college student who had recently been arrested for domestic violence. Through tears, she shared that it was the officer who had first made contact that helped her become whole from the experience and rebuild her life. She had come that day to thank the officer who arrested her for the council she provided her while going to jail and for representing her story so accurately in the police report. Today, this student has graduated from college, completed all of her stipulations from that arrest and now works as a productive citizen helping young people flourish through adversity. Everyone who attended left feeling healed, connected and a part of a bigger community who were all vested in its healthy future.

The ultimate triumph was that our workshops took place the week before the verdict came out in Ferguson, MO that determined Officer Darren Wilson would not be charged for killing Mike Brown, even though he was unarmed and according to witnesses, had his hands raised in the air in surrender. As a result of our workshop, every activist and community member had an opportunity to express themselves in a meaningful dialogue that reduced tensions citywide. While other towns erupted in chaos and protests after the verdict, Corvallis experienced no violence and relatively little push back from the community. Through our workshops, CPD had already demonstrated their commitment to what we collectively defined as community conscious policing.

Shortly after our training, a rogue group of predominantly white college students staged a protest in front of the police station in Corvallis shortly after the Ferguson verdict. Due to our proactive approach to community building prior to the verdict, the NAACP and Corvallis Masons were able to unite together and share with protestors that our police department should be celebrated, not antagonized. Instead, protestors diffused and shortly after the entire town of Corvallis celebrated the positive publicity we all received in the Gazette Times through an article published named, *"Crossing the Color Lines: Police, Citizens talk through tough issues."*

SECTION IV

Implement Solutions

FBI National Academy Associates Community Building Workshop

FBI NAA Oregon Chapter, Portland Police Bureau, Roosevelt
High School
& Center for Intercultural Organizing from Portland, Oregon
- Annual Spring Training

The captain of the City of Corvallis Police Department, David Henslee participated in our Community Building Workshops with CPD, NAACP Corvallis and Corvallis Masons. We did not know at the time, but he and Chief Jon Sassaman are both members of the prestigious FBI National Academy Association. They are the training arm for law enforcement organizations worldwide. In 2015, Dave served as the Vice President for the Oregon Chapter, and he was charged with hosting the Annual Spring training for all law enforcement agencies in the state. By this time, protests and states of emergency had spread to New York for the killing of Eric Gardner by NYPD, Baltimore where Freddie Gray died handcuffed in the back of a police van and Homan Square in Chicago where the police department interrogated witnesses, shackled, beat and tortured potential suspects without booking them into jail. Needless to say, our nation was hurting and desperately looking for an innovative approach to law enforcement training that incorporated community building with an equity focus.

A few months after our workshops in Corvallis, Dave called me and said that he would like to bring his wife to Hillsboro to meet us. We agreed to meet at a local Korean restaurant where we could break bread and catch up. Over dinner, Dave informed my wife and I that he had recommended us to the FBI National Academy Associates for their annual spring training. The board wanted an opportunity to engage with community members versus focusing on tactical training. However, they were concerned with how to recruit and facilitate the event. This would be an opportunity to access most law enforcement agencies in the state. Also, its participants included senior officers who have served as police officers for at least a decade, but most of them consisted of leadership like chiefs, training lieutenants and sheriffs.

The board hired T4T because of our community building component and experiential learning facilitation style. It was imperative that our training be referred to as a workshop since we do not use Powerpoint slides or classroom lecture style explicit instruction. Instead, we create opportunities and questions that enable law enforcement and community to discover solutions to their own problems through collaboration. By the end of our workshops, T4T aspires to blur the lines between law enforcement and community so our bonds may grow deeper and stronger. After dinner, my wife and I accepted the challenge of hosting the annual training for the Oregon Chapter of FBI National Academy Association. First, we had to identify a few challenges before we could develop a plan of action.

Community outreach for our Law Enforcement Community Building Workshops included local and national organizations statewide from the Cambodian Association, National Woman's Coalition, NAACP, Faith Based Communities, Community Citizen Board, Latino Police Commission, Boystrength Program Specialist, Safe Haven, Mano a Mano, Don't Shoot Portland, Homefree, Visioning and Partnership, Youth Pastors, Houseless Activities, Prince Hall Grand Lodge of Oregon, Montana & Idaho, Woodburn City Council and the League of Latin American Citizens (LULAC) to name a few. Community comprising of LGBTQ, representatives who specialize in Mental Health and dozens of volunteers came together to share their vision of *Community Conscious Policing.*

Our team used four sources of data collection to compile this report (Maxfield & Babbie 2005):

1. Written records, such as Law Enforcement Community Building Workshop participant

evaluations from both law enforcement and community members

2. Direct observations and input from co-facilitators

3. Input from Oregon State law enforcement on curriculum design

4. Community engagement and recruitment

Challenges:
- How?
- Mobilizing the community
- Threat to Law Enforcement
- Time and Financial Constraints

1. How?

We were tasked with training 100 chiefs and sheriffs along with 50 community members for 8 hours.

Our curriculum had to be modified to provide a safe space in such a large auditorium with a stage. We had to consider how the room was arranged and how to provide a safe space with so many people. First, we thought it would be necessary to work only with law enforcement in the morning to prepare them for the community building portion of the workshop. The morning, we focused on Best Practices in Community Conscious Policing where nearly 100 senior officers were able to build together on themes such as **Recruitment and Retention**, **Building Effective Teams** and **Community Engagement.**

After the morning session, we broke for lunch and provided it for free courtesy of the Department of Public Safety Standards in Training who funded the workshop. Lunch served as an icebreaker while we transitioned into the community-building portion of our training in the afternoon.

2. **Mobilizing the Community**

Since every officer present would be in leadership and highly experienced, it was imperative that community members recruited be diverse, yet bring the same level of engagement to match the caliber of talent provided by the FBI National Academy Associates.

Following our community building efforts in Corvallis, Hun and I began with our personal networks and invited them to attend. We then trained them as mobilizers to recruit neighbors, members of the community and co-workers who are invested in proactive solutions. Together, we outlined communities who are rarely invited to engage with police and identified organizations that could access them in an authentic way. Through collaboration, I have found that every community has mobilizers or local agencies that are well connected and in tune with the issues that are most pertinent to local law enforcement and the community it serves.

The training was hosted on a Wednesday in Salem, which is at least an hour drive from any major city like Eugene, Portland or Corvallis where colleges are located. This meant that community members we recruited had to

come for free, find their own transportation, take time off from work or school and travel nearly an hour or more to participate. For this reason, T4T recommends that community members be compensated for their insights in order to provide an ongoing dialogue. Since this workshop happened to be scheduled during the state of emergency in Baltimore following the death of Freddie Gray, we did not know until the event if these barriers aforementioned would prevent a significant number of community members from participating.

3. **Threat to Law Enforcement**

We were pleased that 87 of the 100 officers who regis-
tered participated and 47 of the 50 community members
recruited also attended despite controversial current
events. It was interesting that the FBI had received a confidential bulletin that Black gangs like the Bloods, Crips
and Black Guerilla Family had decided to retaliate for the
killing of unarmed Black men by police by uniting
together to kill a police officer. This bulletin was sent
nationwide and deemed to be from a "credible" source.

Growing up in California, my experience told me that in
crisis, gangs tend to unite together to support one
another, their families and neighborhoods. While looting
and violence is promoted through the media, this
description does not account for most young people
searching for a sense of belongingness. If gangs had the
ability to unite together across territories against the
police, most would not wait for a officer-involved killing
to do so. **The Baltimore protests, like others,
stopped when men of color from that particular
community made a visible stand and protected the
officers from protestors.** Gangs united together not to
kill police, but to support their city and comrades. *No
police were killed anywhere in the nation by reported
"gang members" as a protest for the unarmed killing of
Black men during this time.

**Message sent by Law Enforcement in Baltimore,
MD nationwide two days before our training:**

"Baltimore, Md., April 27, 2015 – The Baltimore Police Department / Criminal Intelligence Unit has received credible information that members of various gangs including the Black Guerilla Family, Bloods, and Crips have entered into a partnership to "take-out" law enforcement officers. This is a credible threat. Law enforcement agencies should take appropriate precautions to ensure the safety of their officers. Notification will be sent via NLETS. Further information will be sent through appropriate channels. Media is requested to distribute this information to the public and law enforcement nationwide."

4.   Time and Financial Constraints

By the time Hun and I met with Dave and his wife for dinner to discuss the training, then followed up with the Board to execute the contract, we literally had three weeks and a budget of less than $5,000 to pull off an 8 hour statewide training for 100 Oregon State Law Enforcement leaders and 50 community members. Lunch was provided by DPSST and FBINAA. The first step was to generate a buzz, so we developed an application complete with an overview of T4T and the purpose of our workshop. Utilizing our original Each 1 Reach 1 Teach 1 organizing model based on our personal network, we reached out to a diverse group of organizations and constituents to first recognize the work they were already doing in their respective cities. We also invited them to participate in a statewide conversation with law enforcement by attending our community building workshop near the capital.

T4T Team

Due to the size of the event, we recruited Angela Berkfield, a consultant from Vermont who specializes in White privilege, social justice facilitation and critical race theory. Next, we hired Alejandro Juarez, a Latino man with experience organizing around marriage equality for LGBTQ communities of color and is proficient in group dynamics. For technical and staff support, we hired Nate Okorely who works full time as an engineer in San Diego with Eaton Industries. Finally, Hun Taing came to co-facilitate with us for the community building section in the afternoon while 8 months pregnant with twins! Everyone admired her dedication, leadership and service. We spent most of our budget on facilitators who specialize in the content area and called upon volunteers like Nate and FBINAA board members who assisted in recruiting community members. Collectively, we worked tirelessly to register everyone for the event plus collecting data from each exercise.

Hun Taing, Brandon Lee, Nate Okorley, Alejandro Juarez, Angela Berkefield

Angela, Hun and I met at our alma mater, the School for International Training Graduate Institute, which makes our training network both specialized and global. Collectively, we have more than 20 + years of direct experience and education working in African-American, African, Latino and Asian communities. We are all bilingual and this gives us the skills to connect across cultures and extend beyond linguistic boundaries. Hun is a sociologist by profession with a Masters in Conflict Transformation. She has worked with peace builders around the world and has facilitated mediations on the Cambodian and Rwandan genocides. Brandon earned a Masters in Teaching while serving as a collegiate faculty member and administrator at universities both domestic and abroad. He gained invaluable experience as the NAACP Legal Redress Committee Chairman, worked to establish the Citizens Police Review Board in Oakland, California (2011) and successfully won a verdict through internal affairs against the Berkeley Police Department for police misconduct that resulted in a monetary settlement.

Counter-Narrative of Policing

Based on these initial workshops on a local, then a statewide level, I doubt many law enforcement agencies truly understand that for some community members, police do not represent the *"rule of the law."* The badge represents a form of domestic terrorism to some people like myself who are more likely to be killed by a cop than an extremist terrorist organization such as Al-Queda. In Oregon, systemic bias stem from state based discrimination like the Oregon Exclusion Laws and state agencies, such as police departments and public schools, have the burden of investing in systemic efforts to make a sustainable change with a focus on equity.

Personal Account in Oregon

Within my first 6 months of moving to the Portland area, I had to legally redress Arcadia Security and Patrol at my home, the Hillsboro Police Department that patrolled our neighborhood and the Department of Public Safety who patrolled campus at work. Institutional bias perpetuated through outdated training results in community members like me being racially profiled constantly and ultimately becoming disenfranchised, regardless of where we live in the United States. We seem to always, "fit the description." What I always asked myself working as a faculty member and college administrator in both the U.S. and internationally is why don't I ever fit the description of, let's say, the President of the United States?

Even my wife, while riding the TRI MET Max subway train in a predominantly African American neighborhood in Northeast Portland, was recently stopped, intimidated and bullied by fare inspectors. To make matters worse, she is a fellow city employee and supports law enforcement. This day, it did not matter. While researching TRI MET's training and leadership, I discovered the Commander over TRI MET in Portland Mike Leloff was found GUILTY of verbally abusing a woman desk clerk who worked in his department. She was also a domestic abuse survivor.

The City of Portland paid out $30,000 in damages, including corrective action mandates in 2014; however, Leloff was promoted to preside over TRI MET less than a year later. Due to this lack of accountability in leadership, my wife has now been verbally abused by an officer trained by the same Commander. I recognize a national trend of police who make flagrant mistakes being recycled to neighboring agencies where their disruptive behavior continues against new victims who may not be able to defend themselves. Luckily, our family attorney has filed complaints with several agencies on my wife's behalf, and I am confident that justice will prevail.

It is time that we as a community, including law enforcement, be honest about our internal bias. T4T offers a safe space where we can all identify, confront and dismantle internalized stereotypes while rebuilding a new vision of community together. Without agencies like us, liabilities and violence will most certainly continue to plague our great nation.

Model Examples of Law Enforcement

Agencies such as the City of Corvallis Police Department, Corvallis Mayor Julie Manning along with the FBI National Academy Associates are considered the best at what they do. Training alone is not enough to shift a collective conscious, but it is a start. How do we, police and community, lower our guards to discover the common human experience in all of us? For this reason, T4T's 21st Century Conscious Based Leadership curriculum begins with cognitive development, thereby teaching leaders of

Hillsboro Police Department Community Booth
at the local Farmers Market

all disciplines how to think and approach problem solving equitably. As a result of the fear felt by both law enforcement and community members during this controversial time, FBINAA believed that T4T was the best equipped agency to build a bridge for police and community to open dialogue, heal, share and vision together on a statewide level.

Triumphs

We had the privilege of hosting community members statewide from the Cambodian Association, National Woman's Coalition, NAACP, Faith Based Communities, Community Citizen Board, Latino Police Commission, Boystrength Program Specialist, Safe Haven, Mano a Mano, Homefree, Visioning and Partnership, Youth Pastors, Houseless Activities, Prince Hall Grand Lodge of

Oregon, Montana & Idaho, Woodburn City Council and League of Latin American Citizens (LULAC) to name a few. In addition, we also had members of the LGBTQ community who specialize in Mental Health and dozens of volunteers came together to share their vision on the theme for the day: **Community Conscious Policing**.

Our sponsor was the Department of Public Safety Standards and Training (DPSST) and the event served as the Annual Spring Training for the FBI National Academy Associates Oregon Chapter. We hope that this Law Enforcement Community Building Workshop will become a model that local agencies can adopt to probe deeper into their collective priorities.

While Baltimore was consumed in a state of emergency, students from Roosevelt High School in Portland actively engaged law enforcement officials around the impacts current events nationwide have on their daily lives and how local police can improve relations in their neighborhood through policy amendments, hiring recommendations and budget allocation. For example, one young man said, *"not all young black boys enjoy football, basketball and video games. There are more intellectual ways for law enforcement to engage with minorities such as chess, academic tutoring or consistent mentorship if you want us to respect 'the law' or become cops one day."* How profound.

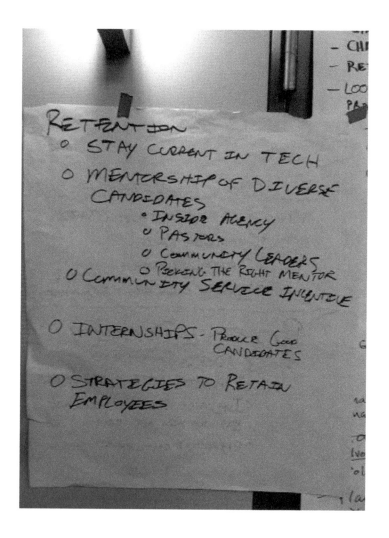

RETENTION
- o STAY CURRENT IN TECH
- o MENTORSHIP OF DIVERSE
  CANDIDATES
  - • INSIDE AGENCY
  - o PASTORS
  - o COMMUNITY LEADERS
  - o PICKING THE RIGHT MENTOR
- o COMMUNITY SERVICE INCENTIVE

- o INTERNSHIPS - Produce Good
  CANDIDATES

- o STRATEGIES TO RETAIN
  EMPLOYEES

SECTION V

Evaluate Results

Lessons Learned

1. Our team was fortunate to have spent so much time learning from a gold star CALEA accredited agency such as the City of Corvallis Police Department. While the size of the department is not comparable to a big city precinct; it does represent many college towns, rural law enforcement organizations that face challenges around recruitment, retention, diversity and community engagement. Because of the support of the Mayor and Chief, we were able to gain complete access to the department, their officers, administration, dispatch and parking enforcement.

2. I learned why many organizations provide diversity training, but nothing like T4T Community Building Workshops. First, the risk involved. Hun and I mediate opinions of others who may be contradictory to our own everyday perspectives. However, law enforcement is not trained to "open up." The 1980's version of leadership based on control is unsustainable. Instead, 21st century conscious based leadership is about recognizing everyone as a living organism and minimizing the carbon footprint we leave after engaging. The choices, rules of engagement and disengagement are more complex nowadays. Law enforcements' linear training methods and tools are no longer proving to be effective when dealing with the community in many cities across America due to the complexities of identity in the 21st century.

3. Today, T4T is training law enforcement how to connect with people they may otherwise have not been able to prior to our workshop. It takes specialized training and another way of processing information to survey one's own bias first, then search for the similarities in others rather than the differences. By doing so, T4T anticipates less liabilities and lawsuits around racial profiling and police misconduct for agencies that complete our certification. Even better, we hope bonds will be forged between officers, leadership and community members that will proactively reduce violence, trauma and pain for everyone involved.

4. I learned that everyone in our workshops is simply responding to whatever trauma, pain or unfortunate circumstance that has impacted their daily lives. Some of us endure more than others. Others of us don't recognize our privileges. The strength is in both community members and law enforcement officers overcoming whatever oppression or barriers that impacted them the most. Discovering the similarities in one another is the most powerful part of the experience. Personally, I learned that the goal of our community building workshop is to end the use of binary language like community members and law enforcement altogether. All of us comprise one community and our language should reflect a co-creative society where everyone contributes to the vision and process.

5. I learned that transformation comes at a cost. For what we offered the state of Oregon, training all of the chiefs and sheriffs statewide, we did it for under $5000. For the City of Corvallis, we did it for roughly the same. Both of these events were service opportunities for us to pilot our curriculum, perfect outreach processes and improve facilitator training. By streamlining costs, we are now in a better position for duplicating our process.

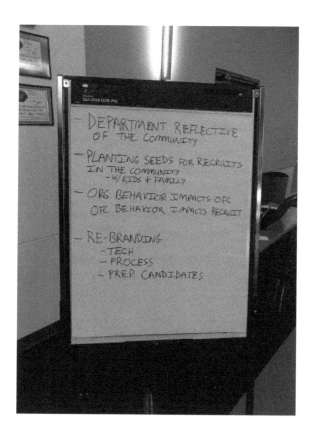

How to Improve

1. Ideally, the innovative T4T training protocol should be implemented for cadets or any entry level candidates into law enforcement agencies. This training would be longer and more intensive if offered through a semester long curriculum where community and law enforcement can engage more than once. Workshop themes would initially begin with examining, assessing and dispelling personal biases. This would involve developing mock scenarios to see what triggers a particular resentment of a group based on race, gender, sex, religion or origin. T4T would go "deep" into examining what makes one feel uncomfortable and why. Issues of race and identity would be discussed. We would also deconstruct the concept of "to protect and serve" with a strong focus on service. Some of the training would initially involve only members of law enforcement and some would involve members of the respective local community.

2. Our training and facilitation methods are based on experiential learning. Expanding T4T on a regional then national scale would require us to increase the number of facilitators and educators in our practices. This would also allow us to improve recruitment, retention, best practices and community engagement.

3. T4T's objective is to acquire a partnership with a national law enforcement agency that can provide the resources needed for T4T to continue their

community building workshop on a larger scale. Having this partnership or even acquiring a government contract will allow T4T to perform with greater intensity.

4. T4T is also looking to establish relationships with communities and law enforcement on a private level. This would mean agencies with residual budgets contract T4T for our services and expertise. The first two workshops, Corvallis PD and FBI-NAA, were pilots to gain experience for our company, so we were glad to accept the terms. Moving forward, we are reassured that there is not another firm in the Law Enforcement Community Service Specialist sector that can compete with T4T in what we do, Community Building Workshops. In addition, we provide institutions with equity evaluations and organizational leaders with one-on-one coaching in order to reduce violence, liabilities and rebuild community trust. T4T does not make any guarantees

5. The City of Corvallis PD experience occurred because everyone at the table consisted of leaders in their respective field who came together for a worthy and common cause, our community. Hun and I not only served as leaders in the local NAACP, but as college administrators at the local university in town. We were vested in more ways than one, and none of our reasons had to do with money or even a business at the time. Any agency that T4T works with has to be a CALEA gold star accredited agency

or very close to becoming one. It's chief and/or leadership need to consist of FBINAA members or have demonstrated some exceedingly high recommendations from reputable agencies and community already. T4T strives to partner with institutions that have a successful track record and are seeking innovative ways to engage with the community they serve.

FBI National Academy Associates Community Building Workshop - Oregon Chapter Annual Spring Training

Vision Statement

T4T is a self-sufficient organization that designs its own contracts and will only work with organizations that are committed to integrity and excellence. Ultimately, we would like to administer certification programs for law enforcement agencies, design our own curriculum for Community Conscious Policing classes in police academies and secure mutually beneficial partnership with community agencies and national organizations. This comprehensive, co-creative process would demonstrate competencies in cultural awareness, sacred service, overcoming the illusion of separation, collective wisdom and authentic community engagement.

Recommendations

1. Offer Annual Certification Programs for Law Enforcement Agencies

    a. Establish a baseline for community building workshops

    b. Conduct an equity-focused needs assessment to define the problem and establish priorities:
        ex. Coalition for Communities of Color
        – Tool for Organizational Self Assessment for Racial Equity
        ex. University of Southern California Equity Scorecard

    c. Evaluate intervention opportunities like new hire orientations, cadet training, law enforcement in-service professional development, school / college campus presence and public forums such as city council meetings

d. Develop an equity-focused community engagement action plan

e. Research and implement equity-focused recruitment and retention strategies

f. Data collection and evaluation to determine best practices related to diversity and inclusion

g. Connect an equity lens to budget allocation for programming and annual performance reviews

h. Develop and implement benchmark goals, including accountability measures

i. Implement a new (or Include the existing) Law Enforcement Community Peace Collaborative

j. Train local non-profit and mission based organizations in capacity building

k. Evaluate Results

l. Develop community building workshop curriculum
   - Tailored for each department and jurisdiction depending on needs assessment (#1b)

m. Professional Development Inservice for veteran officers and cadet training classes

2. Pilot law enforcement training courses and License Curriculum:

a. 21st Century Conscious Based Leadership

b. Diversity & Inclusion

c. Mindfulness Training and Stress Reduction

d. Building a Co-Creative Society

e. Minority Recruitment and Retention

f. Offer Institutional Equity Evaluations

g. Implicit Bias Training

3. Lobby for Mandated Continuing Education in Law Enforcement

    a. Annual professional development centered on Equity-Focused Community Building

    b. As demographics of cities change, residents need an opportunity to re-establish a consensus with law enforcement

    c. Mandate new patrol officers or police cadets to volunteer with local community organizations for the first 2 years (LECC Oregon)

       • Each quarter (every 4 months), officers rotate to a new local agency to discover nuances, insights, barriers to access, struggles, triumphs, holidays and cultural strengths of new residents

4. Offer Community Building Workshops: Half Day (4hours) / Day (8hours)

    a. Train national organizations and local non profit community agencies in capacity building

    b. Train law enforcement in Retention and Recruitment strategies, Building Effective Teams and Best Practices in Community Engagement

5. Encourage politicians and law enforcement agencies to prioritize budget allocation for safe spaces where community and police collaborate regularly on

issues impacting ALL stakeholders in the neighbor-hood, especially residents most underserved.

    a.   Offer paid positions for Citizen Oversight and Police Accountability Boards

    b.   Citizen Police Review Boards should be granted supeona authority

    c.   Chief of Police Diversity Advisory Boards

- Vancouver Police Department Chief James McElvain / Asst. Chief Chris Sutter

6. Present findings through keynote speaking engage-ments at relevant conferences (NACOLE, FBINAA, LECC, DOJ, IACP, DPSST, CJPRI)

    a.   FBI National Academy Association

    b.   National Association for Citizen Oversight of Law Enforcement

    c.   Law Enforcement Contacts, Police and Data Review Committee

    d.   International Association of Police Chiefs

    e.   American Civil Liberties Union

    f.   Department of Public Safety Standards and Training

    g.   Police Executive Research Forum

7. Partner with educational institutions related to social justice or transformative learning

    Ex. Portland State University Law Enforcement Contacts and Data Review Committee (LECC)

8. Campaign Zero: FAIR Police Union Contracts
   a. View Recommendations and Solutions
   b. http://www.joincampaignzero.com
   c. Intergrating recommendations from commu-
      nities research organizations and the President's
      Task Force on 21st Century Policing, these
      policies aim to protect and preserve life

9. Train community in capacity building, legal redress
   and educational advocacy to hold local politicians,
   rogue police officers and institutions demonstrating
   bias accountable
   a. Eliminate Gang Injunctions
      ex. USC Class Action Victory on LA's Contro-
      versial Gang Injunctions
   b. Thamer Valley Police and Thames Valley Sexual
      Assault Prevention Group – United Kingdom
      ex. Tea and Consent Video
      www.rockstardinosaurpirateprincess.com
      #Consent Is Everything campaign

10. Law Enforcement agencies begin tracking excessive
    force incidents and making public all data collected
    related to vehicles, bicyclists and pedestrian stops
    Ex. Berkeley Police Department
    https://data.cityof berkeley.info/

Bibliography

Criminal Justice Policy Research Institute (2011). Decreasing Crime by Increasing Involvement: A Guidebook for Building Relations in Multi-Ethnic Communities. Retrieved from: http://www.pdx.edu/cjpri/sites/www.pdx.edu.cjpri/files/Decreasing_Crime_By_Increasing_Involvement.pdf

Listening Sessions Report: A Community and Police Partnership to End Racial Profiling (2006). Retrieved from: http://allianceforajustsociety.org/wp-content/uploads/2010/04/2006-1004_Listening-Sessions-Report.pdf

Maxfield, M. G., & Babbie, E. (2005). Research Methods for Criminal Justice and Criminology (4th ed.). Belmont, CA: Wadsworth Thomson Learning

Oregon's Demographic Trends (February, 2010). Office of Economic Analysis: Department of Administrative Services: State of Oregon. Retrieved from: http://www.oregon.gov/DAS/OEA/docs/demographic/OR_pop_trend2010.pdf?ga=t2010

Oregon Education Investment Board (2013). Equity Lens Report. Retrieved from: http://www.ode.state.or.us/superintendent/priorities/final-equity-lens-draft-adopted.pdf

Pink, D. (2005). *A Whole New Mind: Why Right-Brainers Will Rule the Future*, ISBN 978-1-59448-171-0

PDX Flash Alert News. (2015). Community Conscious Policing Workshop Brings Law Enforcement and Community Leaders Together Retrieved from: http://pdxfanews.blogspot.com/2015/05/community-conscious-policing-workshop.html

Prengaman, Peter (2002). Racist Statutes Under Siege. Los Angeles Times. Retrieved from: http://articles.latimes.com/2002/sep/29/news/adna-racist29

Thacher, D. (2001). Equity and Community Policing: A New View of Community Partnerships. Criminal Justice Ethics, 20 (1), 1–16. Retrieved August 07, 2015, from the EBSCOhost database

Trojanowicz, R. C., & Bucqueroux, B. (1994). Community policing: How to Get Started. Cincinnati, OH: Anderson.

U.S. Census Resident Population Data. Retrieved from: http://2010.census.gov/2010census/data/apportionment-pop-text.php

U. S. Department of Justice, Office of Community Oriented Policing Services. (2005). What is community policing? Retrieved December 9, 2007, from http://www.cops.usdoj.gov/Default.asp?Item=2624

Walker, S., Archbold, C. (2014). The New World of Police Accountability. 2nd edition, Los Angeles, CA: Sage.

About the Author

Brandon's inspiration to serve as an author and law enforcement community builder stems from his personal experience being confronted with racial profiling and police misconduct on numerous occasions.

In response, Brandon embarked upon a three year mission to support in establishing the Citizens Police Review Board in Oakland, California. His personal complaint served as a catalyst for this unifying effort between PUEBLO, a non-profit organization who advocates for citizen review of police complaints, and the American Civil Liberties Union of San Francisco.

Brandon's commitment to bringing a global perspective to his work began as a student learning a second language. At Houston Baptist Unversity, Mr. Lee double majored in Spanish and Public Policy. Internationally, he has lived in Spain, Mexico, Cuba, Puerto Rico and Japan.

Recently, Brandon completed his graduate internship at La Universidad Autónoma del Estado de Hidalgo (UAEH: University of Mexico) and a private language academy named The Robinson School also located in Mexico through the School for International Training Graduate Institute.

Civically, Mr. Lee was appointed by Governor Brown to the Law Enforcement Contacts Committee (LECC). This organization is charged with assisting Oregon law enforcement agencies with collecting and analyzing traffic stop data, improving community relations, recommending relevant policy and culturally conscious training initiatives.

CPSIA information can be obtained
at www.ICGtesting.com
Printed in the USA
FSHW02n0812070618
49050FS